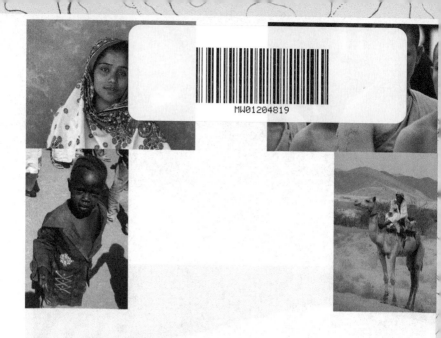

"The things which you have heard from me in the presence of many witnesses, entrust these to faithful people who will be able to teach others also."

- 2 Timothy 2:2 NASB 2020

PRINT FINAL V1.0
UPDATED: 10/25/2021 ENC

INTRODUCTION

Thank you for joining us and many thousands of followers of Jesus around the world in praying for global Church Planting and Disciple Making movements using Disciple Keys.

Over this next year, we hope to take you on an inspiring and challenging worldwide journey of discovery as you are introduced to many people groups who have not yet heard the Gospel message. They represent billions of people.

The title, Disciple Keys, is inspired by Luke Chapter 10, where seventy-two disciples were sent out by Jesus on a mission, two by two. They were directed to find people of peace who would welcome them and open the doors to their homes to host them safely with their families. They were the first church-planters (AKA Disciple Makers)!

Disciple Keys incorporates fifty-two weekly themes with short prayer points, Bible verses and brief introductions to the neediest unengaged people groups. It is available online, in pdf/e-book, paperback and hardback. If you are reading the pdf/e-book edition, this also includes clickable links to more information and online resources.

In Matthew 24:14, Jesus promised that the gospel message would be preached to all nations before He returns. We believe this begins with prayer! Besides praying for those who are not yet reached, we are also praying for workers who have been and will be called to the mission field.

This guide will also introduce you to keys for becoming a disciple maker!

We believe you will find Disciple Keys informative and challenging. Whether you are using this at home, in church, school, college or within a prayer group or mission organization, we pray you will be blessed and encouraged.

Disciple Keys was written by 24:14 Coalition and Finishing the Task, along with several other partner organizations to mobilize strategic prayer for Church Planting Movements.

For more information, to contact us or to re-order, visit:

www.disciplekeys.world

ACKNOWLEDGMENTS

Our thanks to Vision 5:9 for provision of these frontier and unengaged Muslim peoples images and to Ethne Prayer for compiling the lists of Hindu and Buddhist Frontier people groups.

Please write to: engagementreport@vision59.com or visit: ethneprayer.org for further information.

24:14 celebrates our partnership with the Finishing the Task coalition - a movement of organizations and churches working together towards the goal of ensuring that everyone, everywhere has access to a Bible, Believer and Body of Christ.

With the 2000th anniversary of the Great Commission in sight, Finishing the Task is rallying churches and organizations to collaborate in new ways and work together towards broader cooperative goals of a Bible translation for all languages, a strategy to share the Good News with every person, and a church for every 1,000 people worldwide by AD 2033.

To learn more about Finishing the Task and to join the movement, visit:

FinishingtheTask.com

WHY USE THIS PRAYER GUIDE?

"Someone has said, 'When we work, we work; when we pray, God works.' Now work, O God, and glorify Yourself. Amen."

- Mike Latsko, Frontiers USA/Vision 5:9 Steering Team

"Prayer changes history—this is true. The 52-week Disciple Keys is a lovely, fresh-looking resource through which organizations, agencies, churches, and families can engage with God across our world so that many more disciples follow Jesus. People groups representing billions yet to see a church planting movement still have little access to the Gospel. If praying big requests for huge people groups seems daunting, this resource guides you with keys to seeing church planting movements born paired with short bible texts weekly. For prayer that changes our world for eternity, this is an essential tool to keep and use with your Bible."

- Jenny Oliphant, Coordinator of 24:14 Prayer team, Ethne Prayer Team

"It is exciting to see the converging streams of prayer and missions. Prayer is the first domino in reaching the unreached ... prayer leads to vision, vision leads to passion and passion leads to action. Use this guide to daily ask the Lord for the advance of His Kingdom among these most unreached of unreached people groups. The Lamb is worthy of worship from each of them."

- Dan Scribner, Joshua Project

"This prayer guide provides information about some of the highest priority people groups to pray for and good insight about how to pray for movements to begin among them. I highly recommend it."

- Curtis Sergeant, 24:14 co-facilitator

"The destiny of every people group lies in the hands of believers and it must be fought on bended knees as we join the ONE who holds the KEY of Life to unlock the hearts of every precious soul who has yet to hear the gospel! We pray - God ACT!"

- Lucrece Loo, Strategic Prayer co-Facilitator, Malaysia. Ethne Prayer

"What a simple, deep, powerful prayer guide! Imagine millions of us globally praying a key movement verse and principle weekly. Just imagine how God will deepen our prayers and launch movements in the UPGs prayed for weekly (and all the UPGs of the world)."

- Dr. Kent Parks, Beyond, Ethne, 24:14

"Information triggers Intercession, that's the book of Nehemiah. Prayer is the foundation for the Local Church. I am absolutely sure that this spirit filled prayer guide will ignite the passion to reach the unreached in the nations of the world. History is going to change as you pray. PRAY – PRAYER WORKS."

- Minister R Onassis Jeevaraj, Window
International Network

"I draw much inspiration from what I have learned from the Moravians, who understood the importance of continuous prayer to under-gird the church's mission. They prayed around the clock for more than a century and served, giving their all for the Gospel on the mission fields around the globe. My colleagues at International Prayer Connect are reporting an unprecedented wave of prayer being mobilised for mission initiatives across every continent that is producing encouraging fruit including the planting of millions of house churches in some of the most challenging and unreached regions of the world. I commend Disciple Keys to you and trust that your faith will increase as you unlock a deeper understanding of the power of prayer in these times!"

- Dr. Jason Hubbard, Director
International Prayer Connect

CHURCH PLANTING MOVEMENTS EXPLAINED

From the early church in the book of Acts, to the Moravians and the Methodists, to the Naga of India, history has been peppered with large movements of people coming to Christ. Amazingly, in the last 25 years we have seen the rapid emergence of hundreds of these movements worldwide, often in places most resistant to the gospel.

Church Planting Movements are defined as - 'a rapid multiplication of disciples making disciples, and churches reproducing churches, to four or more generations.'

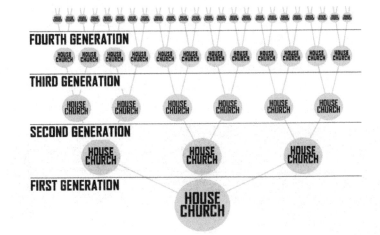

Given the rapid increase of global population, the only way God's kingdom is currently able to grow faster than population increase is through church-planting movements (CPM's)

Part of God's biblical strategy for starting (catalyzing) such movements is through reaching households and groups as demonstrated in Luke 10 where Jesus sent the 72 disciples out to stay with families. (Note the use of the Greek word Oikos / 'family', 'house')

Watch this informative video from Beyond:

https://youtu.be/s-IUraCyByU

PHRASES USED IN THIS GUIDE

DISCIPLE-MAKERS - those who help others become obedient followers of Jesus

MOVEMENTS – Broad description of Church Planting Movements (CPM) and Disciple Making Movements (DMM)

CATALYSTS - a person or thing that precipitates (causes) an event

MOVEMENT CATALYSTS - those God has called to pursue initiating new movements

MOVEMENT LEADERS - those God is using to lead existing movements

INSIDE CATALYSTS - movement catalysts from within a given culture

OUTSIDE CATALYSTS – movement catalysts from a different culture

For more information, resources and links, visit:

www.disciplekeys.world

...go and make disciples of all nations, baptizing them... and teaching them to obey everything I have commanded you."

The Great Commission

HOW TO USE DISCIPLE KEYS

This guide is designed to help you go deeper in effective, life changing, kingdom building prayer for people around the world with very little access to the Good News about Jesus.

EACH MONDAY

Reflect on the Bible verse for the week and the corresponding principle implemented in Church Planting Movements. Ask God to give you His perspective and guide your prayers. Lift up teams of people in cities, towns and villages who are actively sharing the Good News of Jesus. Pray for them to connect with those whose hearts are open. Pray for those who don't yet follow Jesus to ask questions and want to know more about being a follower of Jesus.

CARRY AND PRAY

Download Joshua Project prayer cards to print. Carry the card and pray for the group throughout the day. Share the card with someone else. Invite them to pray for the group, then pass the card on to someone else in similar fashion.

GOING DEEPER

Each people group in this guide was intentionally chosen. They represent large populations of people without enough witnesses for Christ currently living amongst them, for them to hear the Good News of Jesus. They are dear to God's heart, and some from each of these groups will one day stand shoulder-to-shoulder with us before the Lamb of God, as revealed in Revelation 7:9.

To learn more about each people group's lifestyles, where they live, what challenges they face, and what they are famous for, go to the Joshua Project. You can look at the map, do your own research and listen to music on YouTube from this people group. Perhaps Prayer Cast will have a prayer video you can watch, to hear from believers in that nation what life is like and where the needs are to be found.

DURING THE WEEK

Click on the "Learn More" button" in pdf and online versions of this guide to learn more about an unreached ethnic group of people in a particular place in the world. Imagine someone from that group going about their regular life and activities. Ask the question "God what do you see?"

Ask God to reveal to you His heart for these peoples. Pray for blind eyes to be opened, hearts hungry for acceptance and love to be healed, and ears that hear and respond to the Father's calling.

Pray that someone will come and share the truth of Jesus with them. Pray for media and technology to enable them to hear this Good News and respond. Pray hope and restoration over people who have been unaware of God's love for them. Ask Jesus to reveal Himself in dreams and visions, and then send someone to help them understand what they saw.

IN YOUR FAMILY

Pray together at a meal or another family prayer time for the topic and people group for that day.

SMALL GROUPS

Share each week's prayer focus with your group. Pray for the people groups together.

ZOOM

Share the electronic version of this prayer guide and pray together. Unceasingly, over fifty nations and twenty languages pray together through Global Family 24-7 Prayer community around the Throne around the clock and around the world. For information:

https://www.globalfamily24-7prayer.org

To view the schedule and register to join:

https://www.globalfamily24-7prayer.org/prayer-room.html

SUNDAYS

Share the electronic version and related videos during the Sunday morning service. Share the week's topics and people groups via regular church midweek communications, and in bulletin inserts.

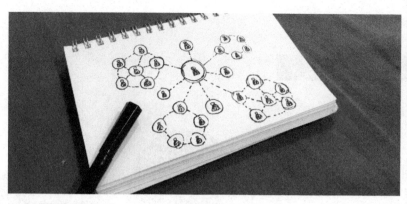

NETWORK

Network with your church's mission outreach and those you know who are working among Unreached People Groups throughout the world. Invite them to spread the word. Ask them to send stories about work that is coordinated with this prayer emphasis to prayer@ethne.net. Pray for missionaries connected to your church.

SOCIAL MEDIA

Share the prayer guide daily or weekly through social media or text message – with your prayer partners, Sunday School, small groups, networks, friends and family.

ETNOPEDIA

Explore Etnopedia. See updates on progress in translating people group profiles into 12 or more languages for the Body of Christ around the world. Help out by recruiting translators to help with this work. Spread the word about these resources to your missionaries overseas.

BEGIN IN GOD'S PRESENCE

Pray for every movement leader and disciple to have deepening intimacy with our Father, and discernment to pray in harmony with His will.

"On that day you will realize that I am in my Father, and you are in me, and I am in you." **—JOHN 14:20**

TUESDAY
GROUP: Buddhist
PEOPLE GROUPS: Amdo, Hbrogpa
LOCATION: China
POPULATION: 750,000

WEDNESDAY
GROUP: Hindu
PEOPLE GROUPS: Brahmin
LOCATION: Bangladesh
POPULATION: 590,000

THURSDAY
GROUP: Muslim
PEOPLE GROUPS: Nubra
LOCATION: China
POPULATION: 700

FRIDAY
GROUP: Buddhist
PEOPLE GROUPS: Amdo, Rongba
LOCATION: China
POPULATION: 163,000

MONDAY

LIFT UP OUR EYES

Pray for consistent and clear Kingdom vision casting and modeling by movement catalysts and leaders. Ask that all in movements love God and others, worship in Spirit and truth, and share the Good News with those who have not yet heard.

"Don't you have a saying, 'It's still four months until harvest'? I tell you, open your eyes and look at the fields! They are ripe for harvest." **—JOHN 4:35**

TUESDAY
GROUP: Hindu
PEOPLE GROUPS: Alia
LOCATION: India
POPULATION: 6,900

WEDNESDAY
GROUP: Muslim
PEOPLE GROUPS: Noorbasha
LOCATION: India
POPULATION: 699,000

THURSDAY
GROUP: Buddhist
PEOPLE GROUPS: Amdo, Rongmahbrogpa
LOCATION: China
POPULATION: 189,000

FRIDAY
GROUP: Hindu
PEOPLE GROUPS: Arora (Hindu traditions)
LOCATION: India
POPULATION: 4,060,000

ABIDE AND BEAR FRUIT

Pray that every disciple and leader in movements would remain rooted in abiding with Jesus. Ask that ministry activities not distract from this.

"I am the vine; you are the branches. If you remain in me and I in you, you will bear much fruit; apart from me you can do nothing." **—JOHN 15:5**

TUESDAY

GROUP: Muslim
PEOPLE GROUPS: Afshari
LOCATION: Iran
POPULATION: 200,000

WEDNESDAY

GROUP: Buddhist
PEOPLE GROUPS: Amdo, Rtahu
LOCATION: China
POPULATION: 101,000

THURSDAY

GROUP: Hindu
PEOPLE GROUPS: Bagdi (Hindu traditions)
LOCATION: India
POPULATION: 2,879,000

FRIDAY

GROUP: Muslim
PEOPLE GROUPS: Ainu
LOCATION: China
POPULATION: 9,700

ENGAGE IN EXTRAORDINARY PRAYER

In every CPM worldwide, prayer has been foundational to seeing a movement started and sustained. Ask God to raise up prayer leaders in every movement and team.

"Devote yourselves to prayer, being watchful and thankful." **—COL 4:2**

TUESDAY
GROUP: Buddhist
PEOPLE GROUPS: Bonan, Tongren
LOCATION: China
POPULATION: 8,000

WEDNESDAY
GROUP: Hindu
PEOPLE GROUPS: Bairwa
LOCATION: India
POPULATION: 985,000

THURSDAY
GROUP: Muslim
PEOPLE GROUPS: Rath
LOCATION: India
POPULATION: 412,000

FRIDAY
GROUP: Buddhist
PEOPLE GROUPS: Bulang
LOCATION: China
POPULATION: 106,000

MONDAY

DEVELOP INDIGENOUS PRAISE AND WORSHIP

Pray that worship and praise in movements would be vibrant and authentic to the movement's culture, growing naturally from local believers as they become disciples.

"He put a new song in my mouth, a hymn of praise to our God. Many will see and fear the Lord and put their trust in him." **—PSALM 40:3**

TUESDAY
GROUP: Hindu
PEOPLE GROUPS: Bania
LOCATION: India
POPULATION: 29,120,000

WEDNESDAY
GROUP: Muslim
PEOPLE GROUPS: Arab, Bedouin
LOCATION: Saudi Arabia
POPULATION: 1,330,000

THURSDAY
GROUP: Buddhist
PEOPLE GROUPS: Bunan
LOCATION: China
POPULATION: 2,300

FRIDAY
GROUP: Hindu
PEOPLE GROUPS: Bania Agarwal
LOCATION: India
POPULATION: 4,836,000

MONDAY

SEEK GOD'S GLORY AMONG THE NATIONS

Ask the Father to give new disciples a yearning to see Him praised –
not just among their people group, but also in every UPG, whether
near or far.

"Declare his glory among the nations, his marvelous deeds among all peoples."
—PSALM 96:3

TUESDAY
GROUP: Muslim
PEOPLE GROUPS: Arab, Lebanese Sunni
LOCATION: Lebanon
POPULATION: 1,395,000

WEDNESDAY
GROUP: Buddhist
PEOPLE GROUPS: Burmese
LOCATION: China
POPULATION: 26,000

THURSDAY
GROUP: Hindu
PEOPLE GROUPS: Bhandari
LOCATION: India
POPULATION: 643,000

FRIDAY
GROUP: Muslim
PEOPLE GROUPS: Asilulu
LOCATION: Indonesia
POPULATION: 10,000

MONDAY

BE GROUNDED IN THE AUTHORITY OF SCRIPTURE

Pray that disciples and leaders in movements will base all actions and beliefs on Scripture. Ask the Holy Spirit to guide them into all truth as they interpret Scripture.

"For the word of God is alive and active. Sharper than any two-edged sword, it penetrates even to dividing soul and spirit, joints and marrow; it judges the thoughts and attitudes of the heart." **—HEB 4:12**; *"But when he, the Spirit of truth, comes, he will guide you into all the truth. He will not speak on his own; he will speak only what he hears, and he will tell you what is yet to come."* **—JOHN 16:13**

TUESDAY
GROUP: Buddhist
PEOPLE GROUPS: Chakma, Daingnet
LOCATION: Myanmar (Burma)
POPULATION: 29,000

WEDNESDAY
GROUP: Hindu
PEOPLE GROUPS: Bishnoi (Hindu traditions)
LOCATION: India
POPULATION: 661,000

THURSDAY
GROUP: Muslim
PEOPLE GROUPS: Budong-Budong
LOCATION: Indonesia
POPULATION: 600

FRIDAY
GROUP: Buddhist
PEOPLE GROUPS: Dawei, Tavoyan
LOCATION: Myanmar (Burma)
POPULATION: 457,000

MONDAY

BE A DISCIPLE WORTH MULTIPLYING

Pray that every leader and disciple would live in a way that would be a worthy model for other disciples. Ask that their focus always be on Christ, not on methods, materials, policies, organizations or the opinions of other people.

> *"In everything set them an example by doing what is good. In your teaching show integrity, seriousness and soundness of speech that cannot be condemned, so that those who oppose you may be ashamed because they have nothing bad to say about us."* **—TITUS 2:7-8**

TUESDAY
GROUP: Hindu
PEOPLE GROUPS: Brahmin
LOCATION: India
POPULATION: 58,787,000

WEDNESDAY
GROUP: Muslim
PEOPLE GROUPS: Komodo
LOCATION: Indonesia
POPULATION: 1,800

THURSDAY
GROUP: Buddhist
PEOPLE GROUPS: Drukpa
LOCATION: Bhutan
POPULATION: 216,000

FRIDAY
GROUP: Hindu
PEOPLE GROUPS: Brahmin Deshastha
LOCATION: India
POPULATION: 568,000

MONDAY

GO OUT TWO BY TWO

Pray there will be no "lone rangers" in movements. Ask for disciples to walk in unity and humility as they work together to bring the Kingdom to new peoples and places.

> *"Two are better than one, because they have a good return for their labor: If either of them falls down, one can help the other up. But pity anyone who falls and has no one to help them up."* **—ECC 4:9-10**

TUESDAY
GROUP: Muslim
PEOPLE GROUPS: Layolo
LOCATION: Indonesia
POPULATION: 1,600

WEDNESDAY
GROUP: Buddhist
PEOPLE GROUPS: Ergong
LOCATION: China
POPULATION: 64,000

THURSDAY
GROUP: Hindu
PEOPLE GROUPS: Brahmin Iyer
LOCATION: India
POPULATION: 309,000

FRIDAY
GROUP: Muslim
PEOPLE GROUPS: Pasemah
LOCATION: Indonesia
POPULATION: 330,000

MONDAY

LIFT UP EVERYWHERE HE IS ABOUT TO COME

Pray for God's light to shine in every dark place. Ask for Holy Spirit discernment as movement leaders prayerfully consider which families and communities to serve.

"After this the Lord appointed seventy-two[a] others and sent them two by two ahead of him to every town and place where he was about to go. He told them, 'The harvest is plentiful, but the workers are few. Ask the Lord of the harvest, therefore, to send out workers into his harvest field.' " **—LUKE 10:1-2**

TUESDAY

GROUP: Buddhist
PEOPLE GROUPS: Ersu
LOCATION: China
POPULATION: 45,000

WEDNESDAY

GROUP: Hindu
PEOPLE GROUPS: Brahmin Mahratta
LOCATION: India
POPULATION: 468,000

THURSDAY

GROUP: Muslim
PEOPLE GROUPS: Baloch, Western
LOCATION: Iran
POPULATION: 2,140,000

FRIDAY

GROUP: Buddhist
PEOPLE GROUPS: Golog
LOCATION: China
POPULATION: 168,000

MONDAY

PURSUE SPIRIT-LED RESEARCH

Ask the Lord to give wisdom as movements research CPM gaps in their regions. Pray for disciple makers to identify spiritual strongholds, dynamics and opportunities in these new places.

"When Moses sent them to explore Canaan, he said, 'Go up through the Negev and on into the hill country... So they went up and explored the land from the Desert of Zin as far as Rehob, toward Lebo Hamath.' " **—NUM 13:17, 21**

TUESDAY

GROUP: Hindu
PEOPLE GROUPS: Brahmin Saraswat
LOCATION: India
POPULATION: 597,000

WEDNESDAY

GROUP: Muslim
PEOPLE GROUPS: Bangobango
LOCATION: Congo, DR
POPULATION: 318,000

THURSDAY

GROUP: Buddhist
PEOPLE GROUPS: Jiarong, Situ
LOCATION: China
POPULATION: 208,000

FRIDAY

GROUP: Hindu
PEOPLE GROUPS: Brahmin Tamil
LOCATION: India
POPULATION: 505,000

MONDAY

PARTICIPATE IN STRATEGIC PLANNING

Pray for relationships between movement leaders as they learn from each other how to be even more strategic in strengthening and expanding their movements. Ask that they make wise Kingdom decisions and plans.

"Surely you need guidance to wage war, and victory is won through many advisers." **—PROV 24:6**

TUESDAY
GROUP: Muslim
PEOPLE GROUPS: Singkil
LOCATION: Indonesia
POPULATION: 65,000

WEDNESDAY
GROUP: Buddhist
PEOPLE GROUPS: Kalmyk, Torgut
LOCATION: China
POPULATION: 194,000

THURSDAY
GROUP: Hindu
PEOPLE GROUPS: Brahmin Telugu
LOCATION: India
POPULATION: 1,046,000

FRIDAY
GROUP: Muslim
PEOPLE GROUPS: Sula
LOCATION: Indonesia
POPULATION: 80,000

MONDAY

SEND LABORERS INTO THE HARVEST

Ask the Lord of the Harvest to send trained laborers into unengaged unreached areas. Pray for Him to raise up harvesters such as the Samaritan woman, Cornelius and Lydia. Pray for Him to stir the hearts of near-neighbor disciples to reach out.

> *"Ask the Lord of the harvest, therefore, to send out workers into his harvest field."*
> **—MATTHEW 9:38**

TUESDAY

GROUP: Buddhist
PEOPLE GROUPS: Khampa Eastern
LOCATION: China
POPULATION: 1,613,000

WEDNESDAY

GROUP: Hindu
PEOPLE GROUPS: Dhobi (Hindu traditions)
LOCATION: India
POPULATION: 11,904,000

THURSDAY

GROUP: Muslim
PEOPLE GROUPS: Topoiyo
LOCATION: Indonesia
POPULATION: 2,900

FRIDAY

GROUP: Buddhist
PEOPLE GROUPS: Khampa, Northern
LOCATION: China
POPULATION: 152,000

RECOGNIZE AND ENGAGE IN SPIRITUAL WARFARE

Pray for the Holy Spirit to give discernment, so disciples are aware of the devil's schemes. Ask for strength and glorious victory as they fight the forces of darkness in their area(s).

> "For our struggle is not against flesh and blood, but against the rulers, against the authorities, against the powers of this dark world and against the spiritual forces of evil in the heavenly realms." **—EPH 6:12**; "in order that Satan might not outwit us. For we are not unaware of his schemes." **—2 COR 2:11**

TUESDAY
GROUP: Hindu
PEOPLE GROUPS: Dhobi Batham
LOCATION: India
POPULATION: 395,000

WEDNESDAY
GROUP: Muslim
PEOPLE GROUPS: Bedouin, Fezzan
LOCATION: Libya
POPULATION: 215,000

THURSDAY
GROUP: Buddhist
PEOPLE GROUPS: Khampa, Western
LOCATION: China
POPULATION: 270,000

FRIDAY
GROUP: Hindu
PEOPLE GROUPS: Gadaria (Hindu traditions)
LOCATION: India
POPULATION: 6,571,000

MONDAY

TRAVEL LIGHT AND AVOID ENCUMBRANCES

Pray disciples will keep their focus on Jesus and expanding His Kingdom, trusting God to provide all they need as they "travel light" and move with the wind of the Spirit.

> *"Do not take a purse or bag or sandals; and do not greet anyone on the road."*
> **—LUKE 10:4**

TUESDAY
GROUP: Muslim
PEOPLE GROUPS: Bedouin, Sanusi
LOCATION: Libya
POPULATION: 650,000

WEDNESDAY
GROUP: Buddhist
PEOPLE GROUPS: Kheng
LOCATION: Bhutan
POPULATION: 35,000

THURSDAY
GROUP: Hindu
PEOPLE GROUPS: Gauda
LOCATION: India
POPULATION: 2,007,000

FRIDAY
GROUP: Muslim
PEOPLE GROUPS: Abai Sungai
LOCATION: Malaysia
POPULATION: 1,200

MONDAY

UNDERSTAND THE URGENCY OF THE TASK

Pray that every disciple would understand the urgency of seeing every people and place reached with the gospel, and pursue the fulfillment of this Kingdom vision.

"As long as it is day, we must do the works of him who sent me. Night is coming, when no one can work." **—JOHN 9:4**

TUESDAY
GROUP: Buddhist
PEOPLE GROUPS: Khmu, Puman
LOCATION: China
POPULATION: 22,000

WEDNESDAY
GROUP: Hindu
PEOPLE GROUPS: Gujar (Hindu traditions)
LOCATION: India
POPULATION: 7,122,000

THURSDAY
GROUP: Muslim
PEOPLE GROUPS: Bilala
LOCATION: Chad
POPULATION: 303,000

FRIDAY
GROUP: Buddhist
PEOPLE GROUPS: Lao Krang
LOCATION: Thailand
POPULATION: 58,000

MONDAY

TRUST GOD FOR PROVISION

Pray that disciple makers will live by faith, believing that when they seek first God's Kingdom and His righteousness, He will abundantly provide all they need.

"And God is able to bless you abundantly, so that in all things at all times, having all that you need, you will abound in every good work." **—2 COR 9:8**

TUESDAY
GROUP: Hindu
PEOPLE GROUPS: Jat (Hindu traditions)
LOCATION: India
POPULATION: 19,103,000

WEDNESDAY
GROUP: Muslim
PEOPLE GROUPS: Bisaya
LOCATION: Malaysia
POPULATION: 77,500

THURSDAY
GROUP: Buddhist
PEOPLE GROUPS: Lao Lom
LOCATION: Thailand
POPULATION: 29,000

FRIDAY
GROUP: Hindu
PEOPLE GROUPS: Jat Gil (Hindu traditions)
LOCATION: India
POPULATION: 234,000

MONDAY

ACCESS BI-VOCATIONAL MINISTRY

Ask the Lord to give disciples in unreached areas creative ideas for making money to provide for their families, while also giving them access to new people and the flexibility to continue making disciples.

> *"and because he was a tentmaker as they were, he stayed and worked with them. Every Sabbath he reasoned in the synagogue, trying to persuade Jews and Greeks."* **—ACTS 18:3-4**

TUESDAY

GROUP: Muslim
PEOPLE GROUPS: Bonggi
LOCATION: Malaysia
POPULATION: 2,700

WEDNESDAY

GROUP: Buddhist
PEOPLE GROUPS: Lao Ngaew
LOCATION: Thailand
POPULATION: 35,000

THURSDAY

GROUP: Hindu
PEOPLE GROUPS: Khati (Hindu traditions)
LOCATION: India
POPULATION: 1,630,000

FRIDAY

GROUP: Muslim
PEOPLE GROUPS: Kiput
LOCATION: Malaysia
POPULATION: 4,100

MONDAY

ASK FOR SUPERNATURAL PROVISION

Ask God to help movement catalysts find and connect the various people and elements needed for launching new movements.

"After Jesus and his disciples arrived in Capernaum, the collectors of the two-drachma temple tax came to Peter and asked, 'Doesn't your teacher pay the temple tax?' 'Yes, he does,' he replied. When Peter came into the house, Jesus was the first to speak. 'What do you think, Simon?' he asked. 'From whom do the kings of the earth collect duty and taxes—from their own children or from others?' 'From others,' Peter answered. 'Then the children are exempt,' Jesus said to him. 'But so that we may not cause offense, go to the lake and throw out your line. Take the first fish you catch; open its mouth and you will find a four-drachma coin. Take it and give it to them for my tax and yours.' " **—MATT 17:24-27**

TUESDAY
GROUP: Buddhist
PEOPLE GROUPS: Luzu
LOCATION: China
POPULATION: 1,500

WEDNESDAY
GROUP: Hindu
PEOPLE GROUPS: Khatri (Hindu traditions)
LOCATION: India
POPULATION: 2,334,000

THURSDAY
GROUP: Muslim
PEOPLE GROUPS: Lelak
LOCATION: Malaysia
POPULATION: 500

FRIDAY
GROUP: Buddhist
PEOPLE GROUPS: Mangrik
LOCATION: Pakistan
POPULATION: 53,000

FIND PEOPLE OF PEACE

Ask the Holy Spirit to prepare the hearts of those who don't yet believe. Pray for God to direct disciple-makers to those He is drawing to Himself.

"No one can come to me unless the Father who sent me draws them, and I will raise them up at the last day." —**JOHN 6:44**

TUESDAY
GROUP: Hindu
PEOPLE GROUPS: Kunbi Anjna
LOCATION: India
POPULATION: 385,000

WEDNESDAY
GROUP: Muslim
PEOPLE GROUPS: Molbog
LOCATION: Malaysia
POPULATION: 8,600

THURSDAY
GROUP: Buddhist
PEOPLE GROUPS: Mangrik
LOCATION: India
POPULATION: 23,000

FRIDAY
GROUP: Hindu
PEOPLE GROUPS: Kunbi Konkani
LOCATION: India
POPULATION: 665,000

MONDAY

GO SLOW TO GO FAST

Pray for those seeking breakthroughs to remain committed to the practices and principles of starting movements. Ask that they not become discouraged as they wait for the Holy Spirit to move in unreached peoples and places.

"The plans of the diligent lead to profit, as surely as haste leads to poverty."
—**PROV 21:5**

TUESDAY

GROUP: Muslim
PEOPLE GROUPS: Bozo
LOCATION: Mali
POPULATION: 331,000

WEDNESDAY

GROUP: Buddhist
PEOPLE GROUPS: Manyak
LOCATION: China
POPULATION: 2,700

THURSDAY

GROUP: Hindu
PEOPLE GROUPS: Lodha (Hindu traditions)
LOCATION: India
POPULATION: 6,608,000

FRIDAY

GROUP: Muslim
PEOPLE GROUPS: Comorian Nzwani
LOCATION: Comoros
POPULATION: 388,000

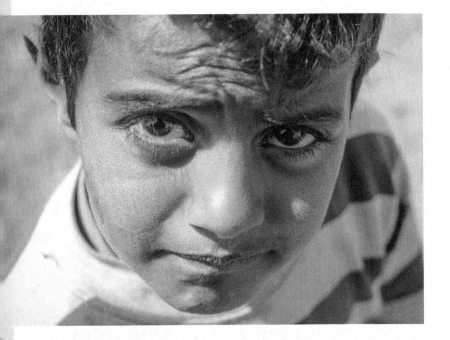

MONDAY

DISCIPLE GROUPS, NOT INDIVIDUALS

Ask the Lord to open households of peace where families and groups intentionally gather for discipleship and learn to obey the truths of God's word together.

> *"Then Peter invited the men into the house to be his guests. The next day Peter started out with them, and some of the believers from Joppa went along. The following day he arrived in Caesarea. Cornelius was expecting them and had called together his relatives and close friends."* **—ACTS 10:23B-24**

TUESDAY

GROUP: Buddhist
PEOPLE GROUPS: Manyuki
LOCATION: Myanmar (Burma)
POPULATION: 20,000

WEDNESDAY

GROUP: Hindu
PEOPLE GROUPS: Lohar (Hindu traditions)
LOCATION: India
POPULATION: 9,443,000

THURSDAY

GROUP: Muslim
PEOPLE GROUPS: Bozo Tiemaxo
LOCATION: Mali
POPULATION: 310,000

FRIDAY

GROUP: Buddhist
PEOPLE GROUPS: Matpa
LOCATION: Bhutan
POPULATION: 20,000

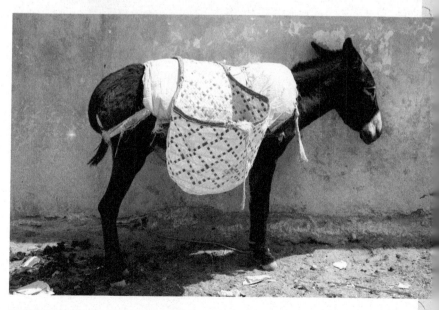

MONDAY

PROCLAIM THE KINGDOM

Ask the Holy Spirit to give disciples words, actions, signs and wonders, to proclaim the coming of the Kingdom with boldness and power.

> "As you go, proclaim this message: 'The kingdom of heaven has come near.' " —**MATT 10:7**

TUESDAY

GROUP: Hindu
PEOPLE GROUPS: Mahratta
LOCATION: India
POPULATION: 30,768,000

WEDNESDAY

GROUP: Muslim
PEOPLE GROUPS: West Marghi
LOCATION: Nigeria
POPULATION: 296,000

THURSDAY

GROUP: Buddhist
PEOPLE GROUPS: Monba, Cona
LOCATION: China
POPULATION: 45,000

FRIDAY

GROUP: Hindu
PEOPLE GROUPS: Mahratta Jadhav
LOCATION: India
POPULATION: 2,781,000

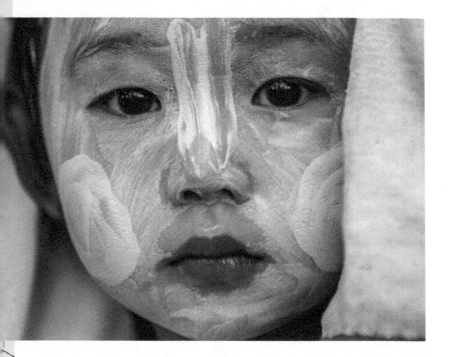

MONDAY

SOW THE GOSPEL ABUNDANTLY

Pray that all disciples abundantly share the Good News in their homes, work places, and communities. Ask the Lord of the harvest to raise up disciples who willingly go into new areas to bring the gospel.

*"Remember this: Whoever sows sparingly will also reap sparingly, and whoever sows generously will also reap generously." —**2 COR. 9:6***

TUESDAY
GROUP: Muslim
PEOPLE GROUPS: Deaf Iranian
LOCATION: Iran
POPULATION: 759,000

WEDNESDAY
GROUP: Buddhist
PEOPLE GROUPS: Monba, Medog
LOCATION: China
POPULATION: 10,000

THURSDAY
GROUP: Hindu
PEOPLE GROUPS: Mahratta Pawar
LOCATION: India
POPULATION: 607,000

FRIDAY
GROUP: Muslim
PEOPLE GROUPS: Baloch, Eastern
LOCATION: Pakistan
POPULATION: 3,800,000

MONDAY

PRAY FOR SIGNS AND WONDERS

Ask that, as disciple makers pray for those in need in the name of Jesus, God would answer with miracles, signs and wonders, and hearts open to receive the Good News.

> *"So Paul and Barnabas spent considerable time there, speaking boldly for the Lord, who confirmed the message of his grace by enabling them to perform signs and wonders."* **—ACTS 14:3**

TUESDAY

GROUP: Buddhist
PEOPLE GROUPS: Mongol, Sichuan
LOCATION: China
POPULATION: 29,000

WEDNESDAY

GROUP: Hindu
PEOPLE GROUPS: Mahratta Shinde
LOCATION: India
POPULATION: 550,000

THURSDAY

GROUP: Muslim
PEOPLE GROUPS: Deaf Pakistani
LOCATION: Pakistan
POPULATION: 2,200,000

FRIDAY

GROUP: Buddhist
PEOPLE GROUPS: Mongols of Henan Country
LOCATION: China
POPULATION: 35,500

MONDAY

LOOK FOR OPEN DOORS

Ask the Lord to lead disciple-makers to households who open their homes and their larger communities to the gospel.

> "When you enter a house, first say, 'Peace to this house.' If someone who promotes peace is there, your peace will rest on them; if not, it will return to you. Stay there, eating and drinking whatever they give you, for the worker deserves his wages. Do not move around from house to house." **—LUKE 10:5-7**

TUESDAY

GROUP: Hindu
PEOPLE GROUPS: Mali (Hindu traditions)
LOCATION: India
POPULATION: 9,897,000

WEDNESDAY

GROUP: Muslim
PEOPLE GROUPS: Arab, Saudi Shia
LOCATION: Saudi Arabia
POPULATION: 2,715,000

THURSDAY

GROUP: Buddhist
PEOPLE GROUPS: Mongour
LOCATION: China
POPULATION: 52,000

FRIDAY

GROUP: Hindu
PEOPLE GROUPS: Musahar (Hindu traditions)
LOCATION: India
POPULATION: 3,014,000

KEEP IT SIMPLE TO MULTIPLY

Pray that disciple makers would go out in humility and simplicity, sowing the Word in ways that are easily reproducible among new believers.

"But the seed falling on good soil refers to someone who hears the word and understands it. This is the one who produces a crop, yielding a hundred, sixty or thirty times what was sown." **—MATT 13:23**

TUESDAY

GROUP: Muslim
PEOPLE GROUPS: Digil-Rahawiin
LOCATION: Somalia
POPULATION: 1,935,000

WEDNESDAY

GROUP: Buddhist
PEOPLE GROUPS: Monpa
LOCATION: Bhutan
POPULATION: 96,000

THURSDAY

GROUP: Hindu
PEOPLE GROUPS: Nai (Hindu traditions)
LOCATION: India
POPULATION: 11,845,000

FRIDAY

GROUP: Muslim
PEOPLE GROUPS: South African Muslims
LOCATION: South Africa
POPULATION: 364,000

MONDAY

MODEL TO REPRODUCE

Pray that fruitful, effective movement DNA is modeled in, and passed down through, every generation of disciples and churches.

> "The student is not above the teacher, but everyone who is fully trained will be like their teacher." **—LK 6:40**

TUESDAY
GROUP: Buddhist
PEOPLE GROUPS: Naju
LOCATION: China
POPULATION: 2,200

WEDNESDAY
GROUP: Hindu
PEOPLE GROUPS: Nat (Hindu traditions)
LOCATION: India
POPULATION: 494,000

THURSDAY
GROUP: Muslim
PEOPLE GROUPS: Afitti
LOCATION: Sudan
POPULATION: 5,000

FRIDAY
GROUP: Buddhist
PEOPLE GROUPS: Ngalong
LOCATION: Bhutan
POPULATION: 88,000

SACRIFICIALLY HELP THOSE IN NEED

Pray for lavish generosity and ample provision as disciples reach out to meet the needs of those around them.

"Share with the Lord's people who are in need. Practice hospitality." **—ROM 12:13**

TUESDAY
GROUP: Hindu
PEOPLE GROUPS: Panika
LOCATION: India
POPULATION: 1,050,000

WEDNESDAY
GROUP: Muslim
PEOPLE GROUPS: Batahin
LOCATION: Sudan
POPULATION: 316,000

THURSDAY
GROUP: Buddhist
PEOPLE GROUPS: Nyahkur
LOCATION: Thailand
POPULATION: 1,500

FRIDAY
GROUP: Hindu
PEOPLE GROUPS: Pasi (Hindu traditions)
LOCATION: India
POPULATION: 7,772,000

MONDAY

MODEL, ASSIST, WATCH AND LAUNCH

Pray for movement catalysts to model healthy leadership, assist new leaders, watch and advise new leaders, and then empower local leaders by moving (in God's time) to peoples and places in greater need.

> "Jesus replied, 'Let us go somewhere else—to the nearby villages—so I can preach there also. That is why I have come.' " **—MARK 1:38**

TUESDAY
GROUP: Muslim
PEOPLE GROUPS: Baygo
LOCATION: Sudan
POPULATION: 1,000

WEDNESDAY
GROUP: Buddhist
PEOPLE GROUPS: Palaung, Pale
LOCATION: Myanmar (Burma)
POPULATION: 292,000

THURSDAY
GROUP: Hindu
PEOPLE GROUPS: Rajput (Hindu traditions)
LOCATION: India
POPULATION: 45,306,000

FRIDAY
GROUP: Muslim
PEOPLE GROUPS: Bederia
LOCATION: Sudan
POPULATION: 1,180,000

MONDAY

OVERCOME PERSECUTION AND SUFFERING

Pray for patient endurance for persecuted disciples. Ask that they look to Jesus for encouragement and as their model for overcoming persecution.

> "In fact, everyone who wants to live a godly life in Christ Jesus will be persecuted." **—2 TIM 3:12**

TUESDAY
GROUP: Buddhist
PEOPLE GROUPS: Qiang, Luhua
LOCATION: China
POPULATION: 25,000

WEDNESDAY
GROUP: Hindu
PEOPLE GROUPS: Rajput Bhatti (Hindu traditions)
LOCATION: India
POPULATION: 875,000

THURSDAY
GROUP: Muslim
PEOPLE GROUPS: Berti
LOCATION: Sudan
POPULATION: 396,000

FRIDAY
GROUP: Buddhist
PEOPLE GROUPS: Qiang, Mawo
LOCATION: China
POPULATION: 21,000

MONDAY
ANTICIPATE RAPID REPRODUCTION

Pray for joyful, expectant faith within movements, to see rapid reproduction of disciples, churches, and leaders.

> *"Now to him who is able to do immeasurably more than all we ask or imagine, according to his power that is at work within us, 21 to him be glory in the church and in Christ Jesus throughout all generations, for ever and ever! Amen."*
> **—EPH 3:20-21**

TUESDAY
GROUP: Hindu
PEOPLE GROUPS: Rajput Chandel
LOCATION: India
POPULATION: 335,000

WEDNESDAY
GROUP: Muslim
PEOPLE GROUPS: Birked, Murgi
LOCATION: Sudan
POPULATION: 223,000

THURSDAY
GROUP: Buddhist
PEOPLE GROUPS: Qiang, Yadu
LOCATION: China
POPULATION: 39,000

FRIDAY
GROUP: Hindu
PEOPLE GROUPS: Rajput Chauhan (Hindu traditions)
LOCATION: India
POPULATION: 3,007,000

MONDAY

MULTIPLY NEW BELIEVERS AND CHURCHES

Pray for the equipping and coaching needed for new disciples and churches to reproduce quickly. Ask that they share the Good News from the first time they hear it.

"Then the disciples went out and preached everywhere, and the Lord worked with them and confirmed his word by the signs that accompanied it."
—MARK 16:20

TUESDAY
GROUP: Muslim
PEOPLE GROUPS: Dair
LOCATION: Sudan
POPULATION: 1,000

WEDNESDAY
GROUP: Buddhist
PEOPLE GROUPS: Qixingmin
LOCATION: China
POPULATION: 6,600

THURSDAY
GROUP: Hindu
PEOPLE GROUPS: Rajput Dikhit
LOCATION: India
POPULATION: 263,000

FRIDAY
GROUP: Muslim
PEOPLE GROUPS: Keji
LOCATION: China
POPULATION: 2,500

MONDAY

FOCUS ON LIVING STONES, NOT BRICKS AND MORTAR

Most movements consist mainly of house churches. Pray that rather than focusing their resources on building buildings, they will continue to focus on equipping disciples as ministers.

> *"You also, like living stones, are being built into a spiritual house[a] to be a holy priesthood, offering spiritual sacrifices acceptable to God through Jesus Christ."*
> **—1 PET 2:5**

TUESDAY
GROUP: Buddhist
PEOPLE GROUPS: Rakhine
LOCATION: Myanmar (Burma)
POPULATION: 2,699,000

WEDNESDAY
GROUP: Hindu
PEOPLE GROUPS: Rajput Gahlot
LOCATION: India
POPULATION: 567,000

THURSDAY
GROUP: Muslim
PEOPLE GROUPS: Khorasani Turk
LOCATION: Iran
POPULATION: 200,000

FRIDAY
GROUP: Buddhist
PEOPLE GROUPS: Shixing
LOCATION: China
POPULATION: 3,700

MONDAY

KNOW THAT EVERY BELIEVER IS A DISCIPLE MAKER

Pray that every disciple maker and leader would catch the vision that ALL true believers have the calling and authority to be disciple makers.

> "When they saw the courage of Peter and John and realized that they were unschooled, ordinary men, they were astonished and they took note that these men had been with Jesus." —**ACTS 4:13**

TUESDAY
GROUP: Hindu
PEOPLE GROUPS: Rajput Garewal (Hindu traditions)
LOCATION: India
POPULATION: 315,000

WEDNESDAY
GROUP: Muslim
PEOPLE GROUPS: Dar Hamid
LOCATION: Sudan
POPULATION: 930,000

THURSDAY
GROUP: Buddhist
PEOPLE GROUPS: Sharchop
LOCATION: Bhutan
POPULATION: 66,000

FRIDAY
GROUP: Hindu
PEOPLE GROUPS: Rajput Gaur
LOCATION: India
POPULATION: 662,000

MONDAY

DEVELOP OUTSIDER-INSIDER PARTNERSHIPS

Most movements have strong partnerships between inside and outside catalysts. Ask the Lord to continue forging many healthy teams like these.

> *"Then Barnabas went to Tarsus to look for Saul, and when he found him, he brought him to Antioch. So for a whole year Barnabas and Saul met with the church and taught great numbers of people. The disciples were called Christians first at Antioch."* —**ACTS 11:25-26**

TUESDAY
GROUP: Muslim
PEOPLE GROUPS: Fezara
LOCATION: Sudan
POPULATION: 410,000

WEDNESDAY
GROUP: Buddhist
PEOPLE GROUPS: Wutun
LOCATION: China
POPULATION: 3,500

THURSDAY
GROUP: Hindusim
PEOPLE GROUPS: Rajput Ponwar (Hindu traditions)
LOCATION: India
POPULATION: 1,259,000

FRIDAY
GROUP: Muslim
PEOPLE GROUPS: Fungor
LOCATION: Sudan
POPULATION: 4,900

MONDAY

BE LED BY THE HOLY SPIRIT

Pray that every disciple and church will continually abide in growing intimacy with God, and serve from a place of increasing dependency on and leading of the Holy Spirit.

> *"When the Advocate comes, whom I will send to you from the Father—the Spirit of truth who goes out from the Father—he will testify about me. And you also must testify, for you have been with me from the beginning."* **—JOHN 15:26-27**

TUESDAY
GROUP: Buddhist
PEOPLE GROUPS: Sinhalese
LOCATION: Australia
POPULATION: 113,000

WEDNESDAY
GROUP: Hindu
PEOPLE GROUPS: Rajput Sengar
LOCATION: India
POPULATION: 400,000

THURSDAY
GROUP: Muslim
PEOPLE GROUPS: Gaaliin
LOCATION: Sudan
POPULATION: 3,935,000

FRIDAY
GROUP: Buddhist
PEOPLE GROUPS: Sogwo Arig
LOCATION: China
POPULATION: 50,000

MONDAY

LEARN FROM MISTAKES

Movements are full of challenges, mistakes and problems. Pray that leaders will be transparent in sharing their mistakes so they can learn from one other. Ask that they live with Christ as their sufficiency and keep moving forward.

"Brothers and sisters, I do not consider myself yet to have taken hold of it. But one thing I do: Forgetting what is behind and straining toward what is ahead, I press on toward the goal to win the prize for which God has called me heavenward in Christ Jesus." **—PHIL 3:13-14**

TUESDAY
GROUP: Hindu
PEOPLE GROUPS: Tamboli (Hindu traditions)
LOCATION: India
POPULATION: 1,856,000

WEDNESDAY
GROUP: Muslim
PEOPLE GROUPS: Gawamaa
LOCATION: Sudan
POPULATION: 1,225,000

THURSDAY
GROUP: Buddhist
PEOPLE GROUPS: Tai Khang
LOCATION: Laos
POPULATION: 26,000

FRIDAY
GROUP: Hindu
PEOPLE GROUPS: Teli (Hindu traditions)
LOCATION: India
POPULATION: 18,686,000

MONDAY

UNDERSTAND THAT CHURCH IS FAMILY

Pray for strong relationships and loyalty to mark the church. Ask that the church work together as family, care for one another, and reach out to those who have not yet heard the Good News.

"Be devoted to one another in love. Honor one another above yourselves."
—ROM 12:10

TUESDAY
GROUP: Muslim
PEOPLE GROUPS: Gimma
LOCATION: Sudan
POPULATION: 198,000

WEDNESDAY
GROUP: Buddhist
PEOPLE GROUPS: Tai lue
LOCATION: Laos
POPULATION: 129,000

THURSDAY
GROUP: Hindu
PEOPLE GROUPS: Thakkar
LOCATION: India
POPULATION: 583,000

FRIDAY
GROUP: Muslm
PEOPLE GROUPS: Guhayna
LOCATION: Sudan
POPULATION: 1,805,000

MONDAY

DISTRIBUTE "HOT COALS"

Ask God to bless an intentional "hot coals" strategy where disciples in a movement move to an unengaged unreached people or place where they have some kind of connection (e.g. family tie, near culture).

> *"But you will receive power when the Holy Spirit comes on you; and you will be my witnesses in Jerusalem, and in all Judea and Samaria, and to the ends of the earth."* —**ACTS 1:8**

TUESDAY

GROUP: Buddhist
PEOPLE GROUPS: Yugur, Enger
LOCATION: China
POPULATION: 6,100

WEDNESDAY

GROUP: Hindu
PEOPLE GROUPS: Vaddar (Hindu traditions)
LOCATION: India
POPULATION: 3,604,000

THURSDAY

GROUP: Muslim
PEOPLE GROUPS: Laki
LOCATION: Iran
POPULATION: 1,000,000

FRIDAY

GROUP: Buddhist
PEOPLE GROUPS: Tebbu
LOCATION: China
POPULATION: 26,000

MONDAY

TRAIN AND RELEASE

Pray that movement leaders will release into new areas those trained in CPM principles. Pray for growing networking and collaboration between movements.

*"While they were worshiping the Lord and fasting, the Holy Spirit said, 'Set apart for me Barnabas and Saul for the work to which I have called them.' So after they had fasted and prayed, they placed their hands on them and sent them off." —***ACTS 13:2-3**

TUESDAY
GROUP: Hindu
PEOPLE GROUPS: Vanjara
LOCATION: India
POPULATION: 952,000

WEDNESDAY
GROUP: Muslim
PEOPLE GROUPS: Hasania
LOCATION: Sudan
POPULATION: 917,000

THURSDAY
GROUP: Buddhist
PEOPLE GROUPS: Thai, Northern
LOCATION: Laos
POPULATION: 37,000

FRIDAY
GROUP: Hindu
PEOPLE GROUPS: Yadav (Hindu traditions)
LOCATION: India
POPULATION: 58,320,000

MONDAY

DIE TO SELF

Pray that every disciple and movement leader will intentionally and consistently die to themselves in order to see multiplication in movements.

"Very truly I tell you, unless a kernel of wheat falls to the ground and dies, it remains only a single seed. But if it dies, it produces many seeds." **—JOHN 12:24**

TUESDAY
GROUP: Muslim
PEOPLE GROUPS: Husseinat
LOCATION: Sudan
POPULATION: 201,000

WEDNESDAY
GROUP: Buddhist
PEOPLE GROUPS: Yugur, Saragh
LOCATION: China
POPULATION: 9,000

THURSDAY
GROUP: Hindu
PEOPLE GROUPS: Yadav (Hindu traditions)
LOCATION: Nepal
POPULATION: 1,006,000

FRIDAY
GROUP: Muslim
PEOPLE GROUPS: Luwu
LOCATION: Indonesia
POPULATION: 290,000

MONDAY

MONDAY

MOVE WITH THE MOVERS

Pray that leaders will invest the majority of their time with those who are obeying God's word ("move with the movers; don't linger with the lingerers").

> *"When he arrived at the house of Jairus, he did not let anyone go in with him except Peter, John and James, and the child's father and mother."* —**LUKE 8:51**, *"Meanwhile, when a crowd of many thousands had gathered, so that they were trampling on one another, Jesus began to speak first to his disciples, saying: 'Be[a] on your guard against the yeast of the Pharisees, which is hypocrisy.' "* —**LUKE 12:1**

TUESDAY
GROUP: Buddhist
PEOPLE GROUPS: Tibetan Gtsang
LOCATION: China
POPULATION: 766,000

WEDNESDAY
GROUP: Hindu
PEOPLE GROUPS: Yadav Gualbans (Hindu traditions)
LOCATION: Nepal
POPULATION: 28,000

THURSDAY
GROUP: Muslim
PEOPLE GROUPS: Kawahia
LOCATION: Sudan
POPULATION: 1,100,000

FRIDAY
GROUP: Buddhist
PEOPLE GROUPS: Tibetan, Central
LOCATION: China
POPULATION: 949,000

MONDAY

WALK IN HUMILITY

Ask the Lord to empower all disciples and movement leaders to walk in humility, putting others ahead of themselves.

> *"Do nothing out of selfish ambition or vain conceit. Rather, in humility value others above yourselves, not looking to your own interests but each of you to the interests of the others."* **—PHIL 2:3-4**

TUESDAY

GROUP: Hindu
PEOPLE GROUPS: Banjara (Hindu traditions)
LOCATION: Pakistan
POPULATION: 153,000

WEDNESDAY

GROUP: Muslim
PEOPLE GROUPS: Keiga Jirru
LOCATION: Sudan
POPULATION: 1,400

THURSDAY

GROUP: Buddhist
PEOPLE GROUPS: Tibetan, Nghari
LOCATION: China
POPULATION: 64,000

FRIDAY

GROUP: Hindu
PEOPLE GROUPS: Gujarati, Ugandan
LOCATION: Uganda
POPULATION: 465,000

MONDAY

REGULARLY REVIEW, REVISE AND REGROUP

Ask God to give movement coaches and disciple makers vision and courage to evaluate the work regularly and clearly see what needs to be continued, started, changed or stopped.

"Brothers and sisters, I do not consider myself yet to have taken hold of it. But one thing I do: Forgetting what is behind and straining toward what is ahead, I press on toward the goal to win the prize for which God has called me heavenward in Christ Jesus." **—PHIL 3:13-14**

TUESDAY
GROUP: Muslim
PEOPLE GROUPS: Kimr
LOCATION: Sudan
POPULATION: 201,000

WEDNESDAY
GROUP: Buddhist
PEOPLE GROUPS: Tibetan, Shanyan
LOCATION: China
POPULATION: 26,000

THURSDAY
GROUP: Hindu
PEOPLE GROUPS: Gujarati
LOCATION: United Kingdom
POPULATION: 635,000

FRIDAY
GROUP: Muslim
PEOPLE GROUPS: Lafofa
LOCATION: Sudan
POPULATION: 7,400

MONDAY

FOCUS ON THE GAPS

Ask the Lord to open doors for the gospel, and open the spiritual eyes of each believer. Pray for every church to play a part in filling gaps where there is not yet CPM engagement.

> "It has always been my ambition to preach the gospel where Christ was not known, so that I would not be building on someone else's foundation. Rather, as it is written: 'Those who were not told about him will see, and those who have not heard will understand.' " **—ROMANS 15:20-21**

TUESDAY

GROUP: Buddhist
PEOPLE GROUPS: Tibetan, Zhugqu
LOCATION: China
POPULATION: 50,000

WEDNESDAY

GROUP: Muslim
PEOPLE GROUPS: Lahawin
LOCATION: Sudan
POPULATION: 231,000

THURSDAY

GROUP: Buddhist
PEOPLE GROUPS: Tu
LOCATION: China
POPULATION: 262,000

FRIDAY

GROUP: Muslim
PEOPLE GROUPS: Logoi
LOCATION: Sudan
POPULATION: 12,500

MONDAY

GIVE THANKS IN EVERYTHING

Pray that from the very beginning disciple makers would establish in movements the DNA of thankfulness in all circumstances.

> "Give thanks in all circumstances; for this is God's will for you in Christ Jesus."
> **—1 THES 5:18**

TUESDAY
GROUP: Buddhist
PEOPLE GROUPS: Za
LOCATION: China
POPULATION: 3,300

WEDNESDAY
GROUP: Muslim
PEOPLE GROUPS: Qizilbash
LOCATION: Afghanistan
POPULATION: 200,000

THURSDAY
GROUP: Buddhist
PEOPLE GROUPS: Yaw
LOCATION: Myanmar (Burma)
POPULATION: 22,000

FRIDAY
GROUP: Muslim
PEOPLE GROUPS: Miri
LOCATION: Sudan
POPULATION: 4,300

MONDAY

HAVE FAITH AND PERSEVERE

Ask the Father to give disciples unshakable faith in Him, and in His promises, that will carry them through every difficulty and hardship.

"We want each of you to show this same diligence to the very end, so that what you hope for may be fully realized. We do not want you to become lazy, but to imitate those who through faith and patience inherit what has been promised."
—HEB 6:11-12

TUESDAY
GROUP: Buddhist
PEOPLE GROUPS: Saek
LOCATION: Thailand
POPULATION: 21,000

WEDNESDAY
GROUP: Muslim
PEOPLE GROUPS: Rizeiqat
LOCATION: Sudan
POPULATION: 478,000

THURSDAY
GROUP: Buddhist
PEOPLE GROUPS: Tai Lue
LOCATION: Thailand
POPULATION: 91,000

FRIDAY
GROUP: Muslim
PEOPLE GROUPS: Sherifi
LOCATION: Sudan
POPULATION: 232,000

MOVEMENTS START NEW MOVEMENTS

Over 80% of movements are started by other movements. Pray for movement leaders to collaborate well together as they lead their movements in finding the best strategies for starting new movements.

"As iron sharpens iron so one person sharpens another." **—PROV 27:17**

TUESDAY
GROUP: Buddhist
PEOPLE GROUPS: Thai, Tak Bai
LOCATION: Thailand
POPULATION: 22,000

WEDNESDAY
GROUP: Muslim
PEOPLE GROUPS: Shukria
LOCATION: Sudan
POPULATION: 332,000

THURSDAY
GROUP: Muslim
PEOPLE GROUPS: Shina
LOCATION: Pakistan
POPULATION: 657,000

FRIDAY
GROUP: Muslim
PEOPLE GROUPS: Tese
LOCATION: Sudan
POPULATION: 1,400

MONDAY

PURSUE UNITY AMONG BELIEVERS

Pray that disciples, movement leaders and the global body of Christ will walk in love and unity as we seek to fulfill Matthew 24:14.

> *"May the God who gives endurance and encouragement give you the same attitude of mind toward each other that Christ Jesus had, so that with one mind and one voice you may glorify the God and Father of our Lord Jesus Christ."*
> **—ROM 15:5-6**

TUESDAY
GROUP: Muslim
PEOPLE GROUPS: Tumale
LOCATION: Sudan
POPULATION: 19,000

WEDNESDAY
GROUP: Muslim
PEOPLE GROUPS: Warnang
LOCATION: Sudan
POPULATION: 1,100

THURSDAY
GROUP: Muslim
PEOPLE GROUPS: Yazeed
LOCATION: Sudan
POPULATION: 526,000

FRIDAY
GROUP: Muslim
PEOPLE GROUPS: Shiites
LOCATION: Syria
POPULATION: 1,140,000

MONDAY

SHARE EFFECTIVELY WITH MANY PEOPLE

Ask the Lord to raise up more disciples who share effectively with many people, like the healed demoniac in Mark 5 and the Samaritan woman in John 4.

—MARK 5, JOHN 4

TUESDAY
GROUP: Muslim
PEOPLE GROUPS: Mwera
LOCATION: Tanzania
POPULATION: 735,000

WEDNESDAY
GROUP: Muslim
PEOPLE GROUPS: Zigua
LOCATION: Tanzania
POPULATION: 693,000

THURSDAY
GROUP: Muslim
PEOPLE GROUPS: Turk
LOCATION: India
POPULATION: 331,000

FRIDAY
GROUP: Muslim
PEOPLE GROUPS: Kotokoli
LOCATION: Togo
POPULATION: 239,000

MONDAY

EXPERIENCE SEASONS OF PEACE AND FRUITFULNESS

Pray for seasons of peace, sustained fruitfulness, and encouragement as disciples and churches continue to work to reach every unreached people and place.

> "Then the church throughout Judea, Galilee and Samaria enjoyed a time of peace and was strengthened. Living in the fear of the Lord and encouraged by the Holy Spirit, it increased in numbers." —**ACTS 9:31**

TUESDAY
GROUP: Muslim
PEOPLE GROUPS: Akhdam
LOCATION: Yemen
POPULATION: 1,645,000

WEDNESDAY
GROUP: Muslim
PEOPLE GROUPS: Arab, Northern Yemeni
LOCATION: Yemen
POPULATION: 11,890,000

THURSDAY
GROUP: Muslim
PEOPLE GROUPS: Arab, Tihama Yemeni
LOCATION: Yemen
POPULATION: 5,040,000

FRIDAY
GROUP: Buddhist
PEOPLE GROUPS: Amdo, Hbrogpa
LOCATION: China
POPULATION: 750,000

THANK YOU
TO OUR PARTNERS!

Made in the USA
Columbia, SC
13 November 2021